Norman Gnome
Knows
All Of
The
ABC's!

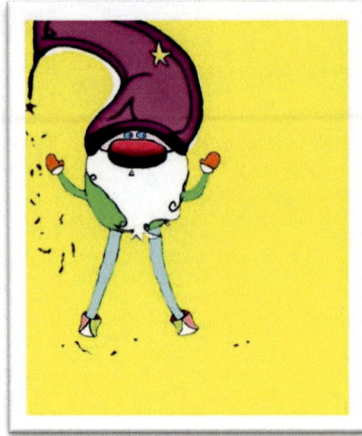

Norman Gnome Knows All Of The ABC's!

Written and Illustrated by Roberta M. Griffis, B.S.Ed.

Cover by RG Artfelt

www.RGArtfelt.com

Published in the United States of America

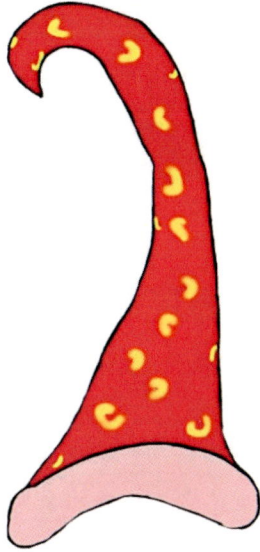

This book belongs to:

_____

Meet
Norman
Gnome

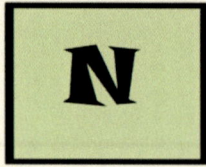

Some lowercase letters are short.

a c e i m n o

r s u v w x z

Some lowercase letters have a tail.

g j p q y

Some lowercase letters are tall.

b d f h k l t

Not one of the uppercase letters are small.

A B C D E F G H

I J K L M N

O P Q R S T U V

W X Y Z

Norman Gnome says, "Tail or no, small or tall, turn the page and we will write them all!"

ABCDEFGHIJKLMNOPQRSTUVWXYZ

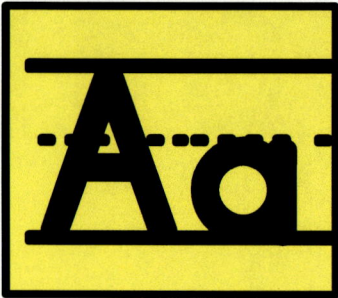

abcdefghijklmnopqrstuvwxyz

A is for **a**nt.
Run **a**way if you
see **a** red fire **a**nt!

Trace all of the letters then write your own.

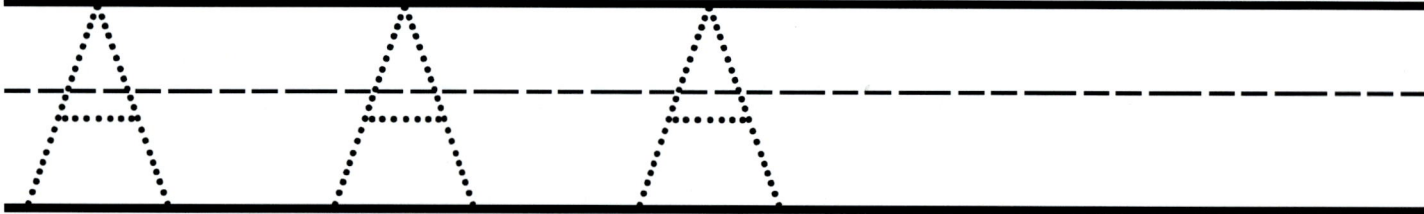

A A A

a a a

Trace then say the missing letters.

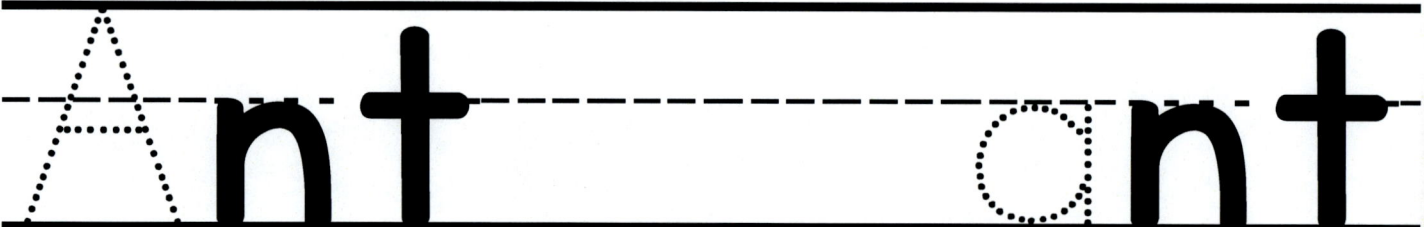

Ant   ont

ABCDEFGHIJKLMNOPQRSTUVWXYZ
abcdefghijklmnopqrstuvwxyz

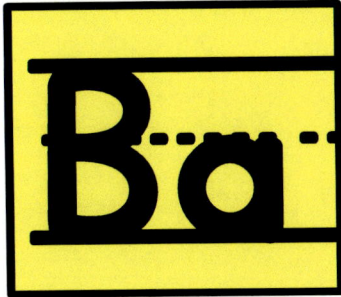

B is for **b**at.
Norman Gnome has
one **b**lue **b**ase**b**all **b**at.

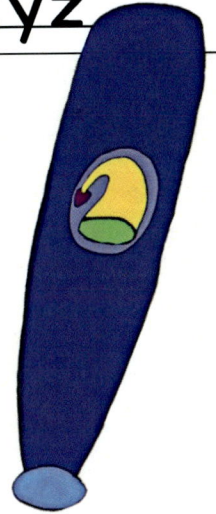

Trace all of the letters then write your own.

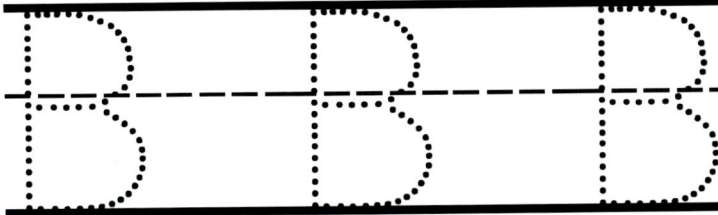

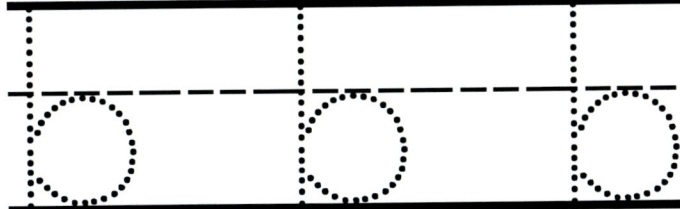

Trace then say the missing letters.

ABCDEFGHIJKLMNOPQRSTUVWXYZ

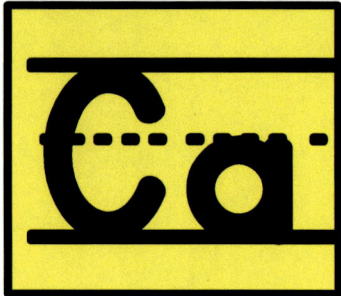

abcdefghijklmnopqrstuvwxyz

C is for **clock.**

Ti**c**k to**c**k **c**li**c**ks the **c**ir**c**le **c**lo**c**k.

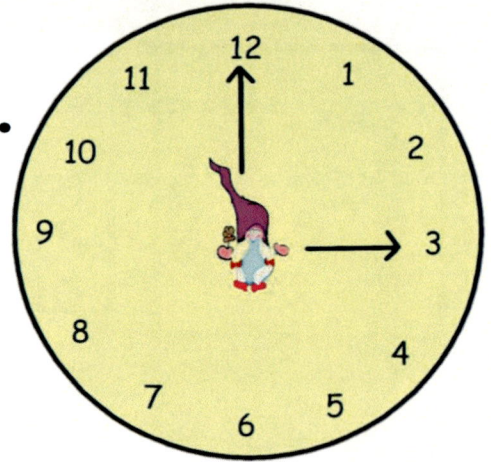

Trace all of the letters then write your own.

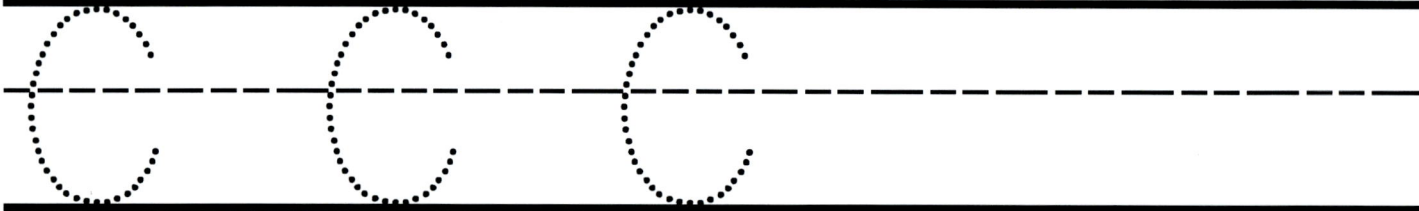

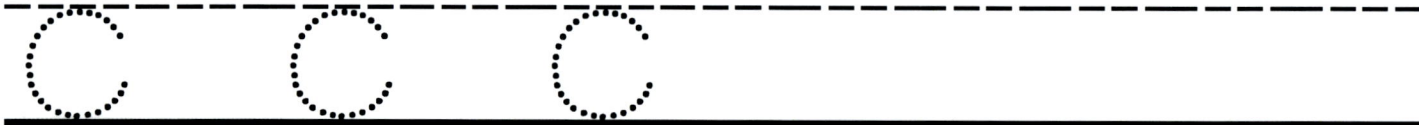

C C C

c c c

Trace then say the missing letters.

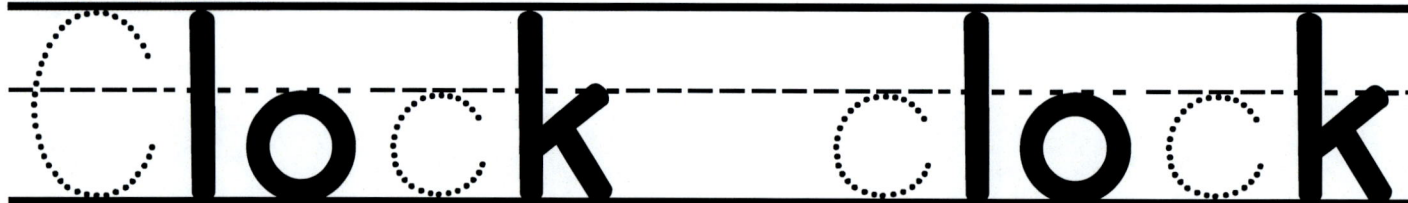

clock clock

ABCD EFGHIJKLMNOPQRSTUVWXYZ

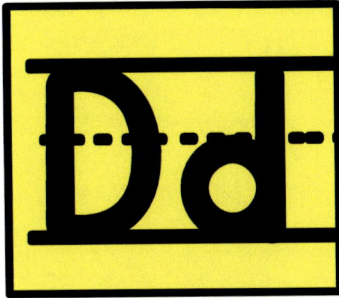

abcdefghijklmnopqrstuvwxyz

D is for **d**aisy.
A single **d**elicate
dainty **d**aisy.

Trace all of the letters then write your own.

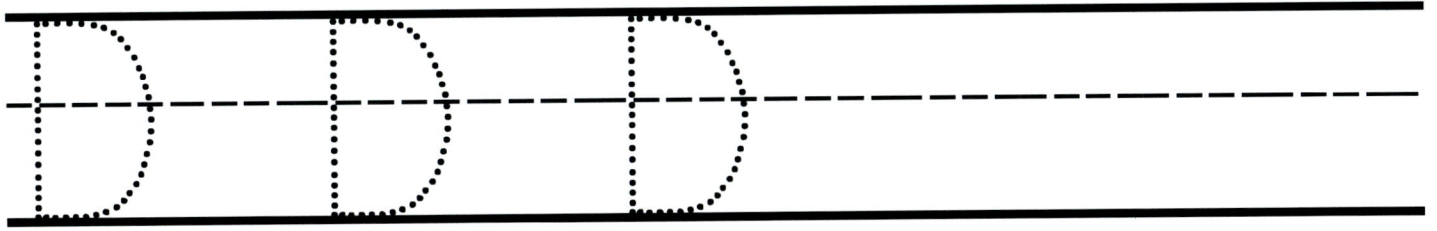

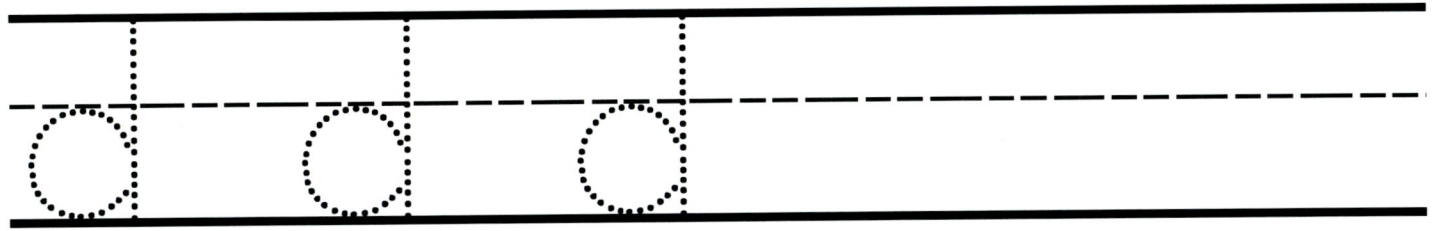

D   D   D

d   d   d

Trace then say the missing letters.

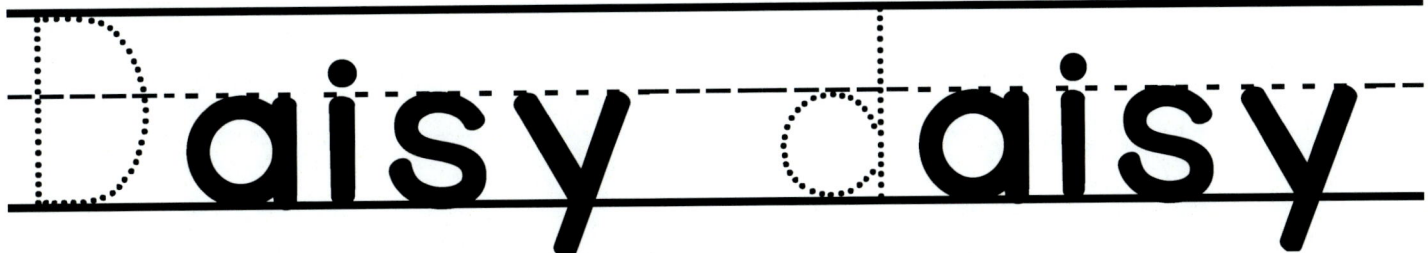

Daisy daisy

ABCD**E**FGHIJKLMNOPQRSTUVWXYZ

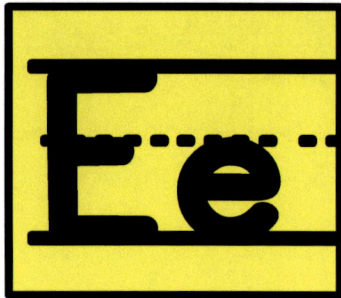

abcd**e**fghijklmnopqrstuvwxyz

Ee

E is for **e**lf.
Elsi**e** **E**lf has
bright gr**ee**n **e**y**e**s.

Trace all of the letters then write your own.

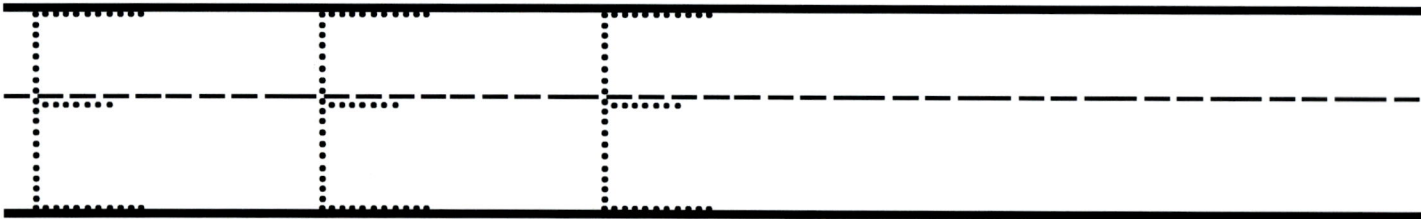

E   E   E

e   e   e

Trace then say the missing letters.

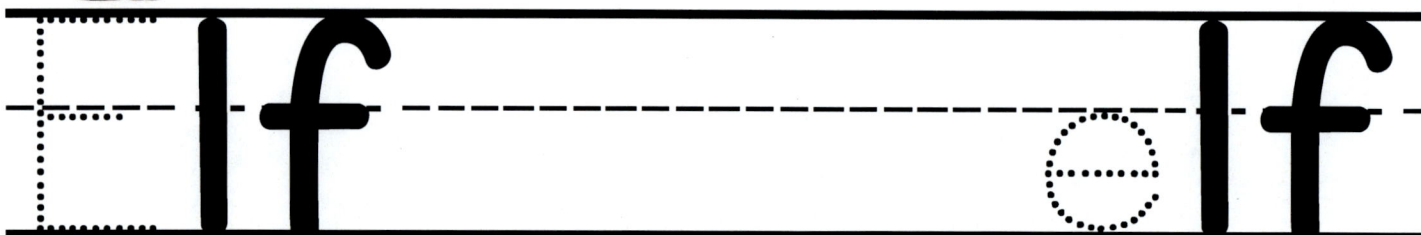

Elf   elf

ABCDE**F**GHIJKLMNOPQRSTUVWXYZ

abcde**f**ghijklmnopqrstuvwxyz

F f

F is **f**or **f**our.
Four **f**ine **f**riends
having **f**un.

Trace all the letters then write your own.

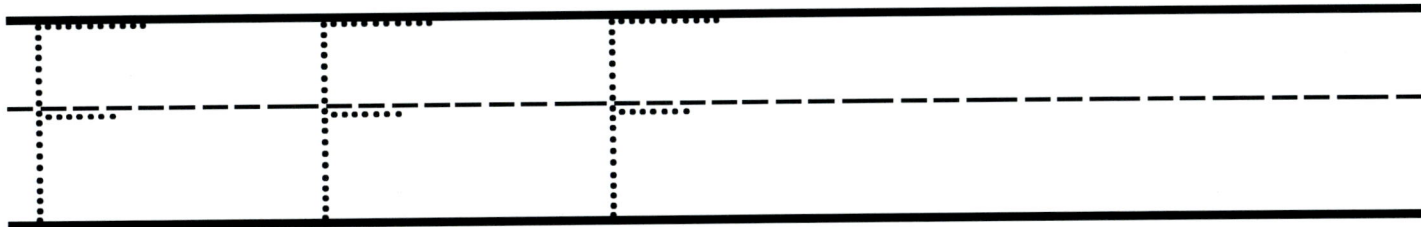

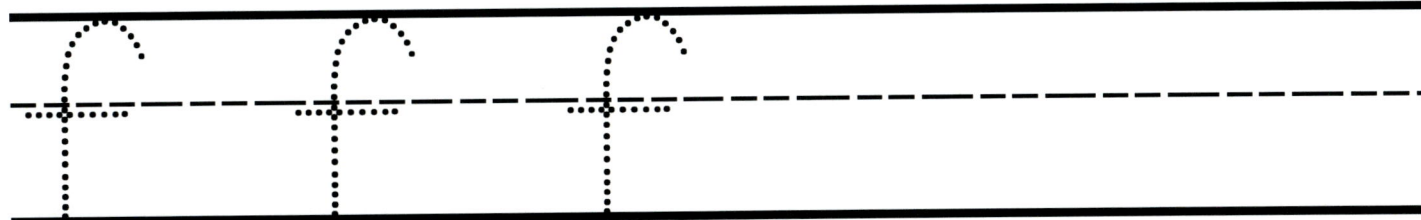

F F F

f f f

Trace then say the missing letters.

our f our

ABCDEF**G**HIJKLMNOPQRSTUVWXYZ

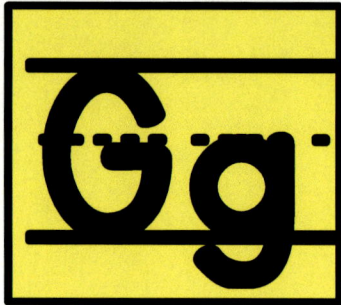

abcdef**g**hijklmnopqrstuvwxyz

Gg

G is for **g**roup.
A **g**roup of
slu**gg**y slu**g**s.

Trace all of the letters then write your own.

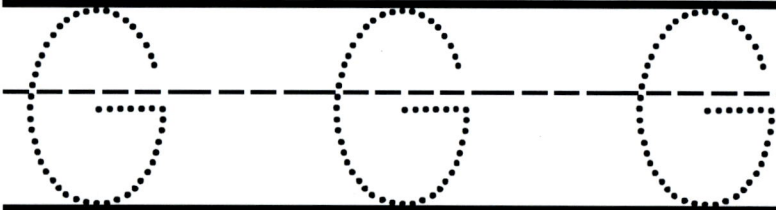

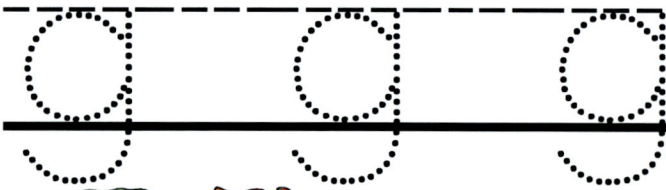

G   G   G

g   g   g

Trace then say the missing letters.

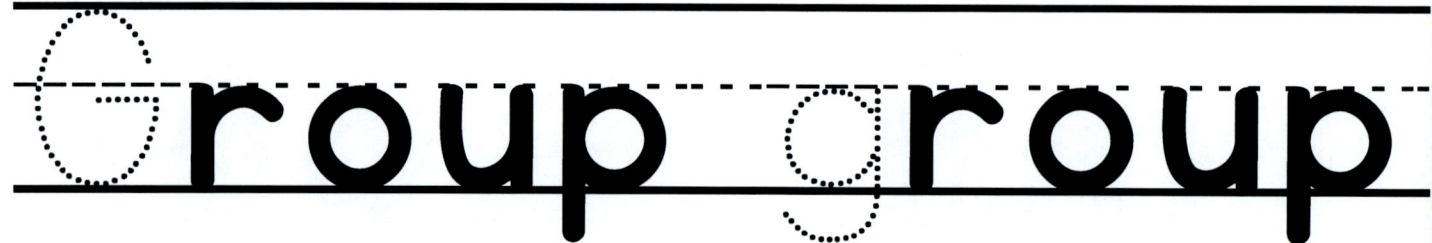

Group group

ABCDEFG**H**IJKLMNOPQRSTUVWXYZ

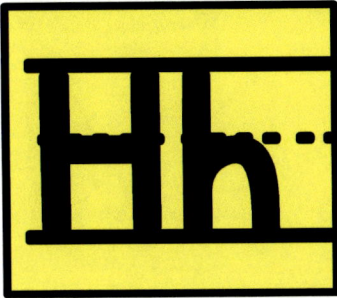

abcdefg**h**ijklmnopqrstuvwxyz

Hh

H is for **h**ats.
Three bright **h**ats
to wear upon your **h**ead.

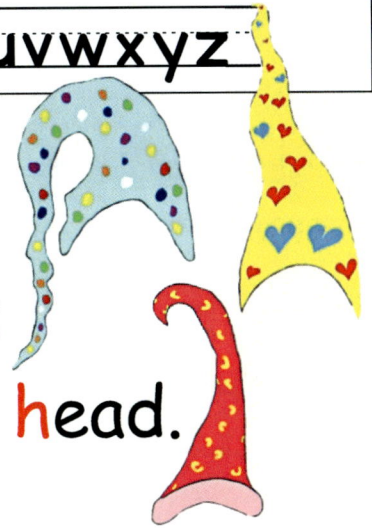

Trace all of the letters then write your own.

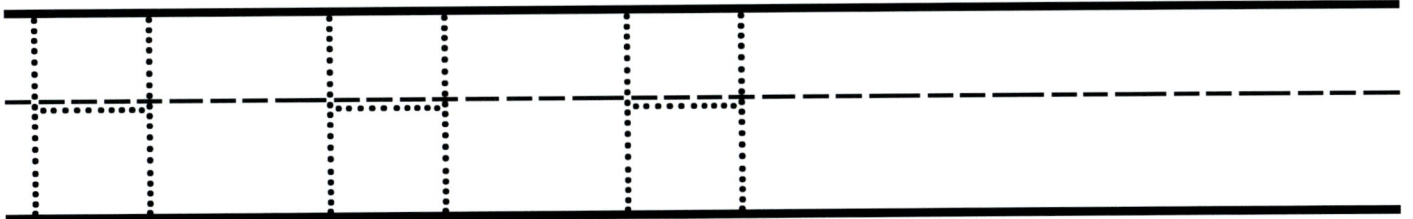

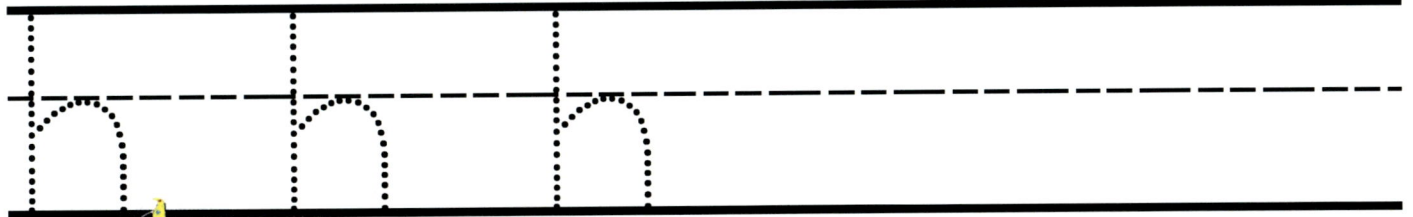

Trace then say the missing letters.

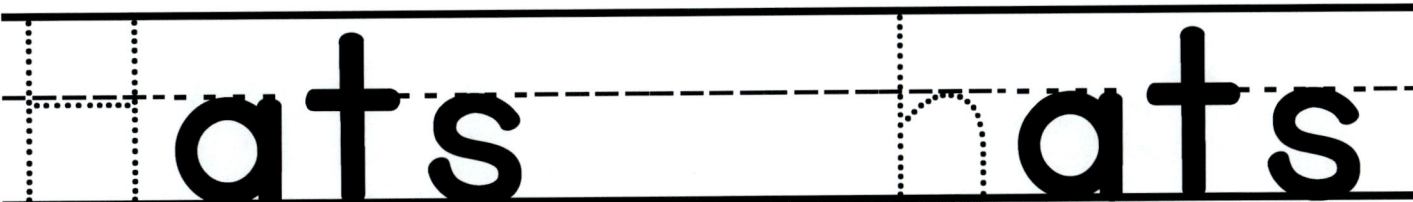

Hats hats

ABCDEFGH**I**JKLMNOPQRSTUVWXYZ

abcdefgh**i**jklmnopqrstuvwxyz

I is for **i**ce.
A cube of **i**ce
is qu**i**te ch**i**lly!

Trace all of the letters then write your own.

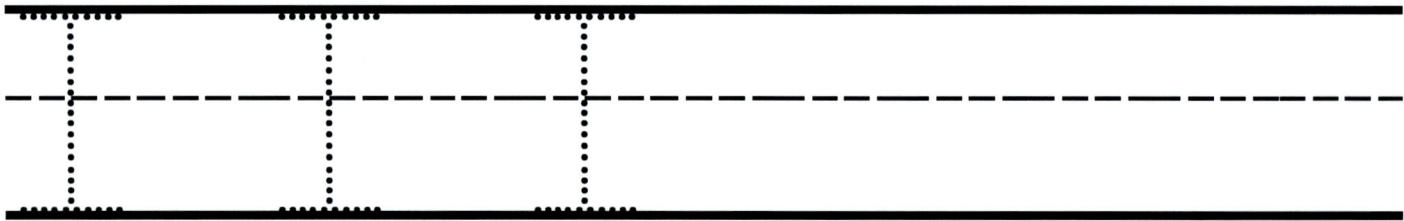

Trace then say the missing letters.

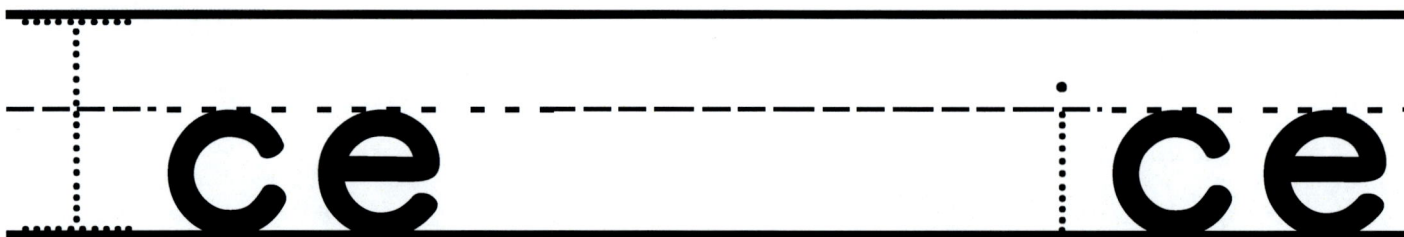

ice **i**ce

ABCDEFGHI**J**KLMNOPQRSTUVWXYZ

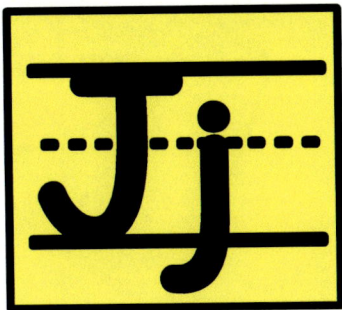

abcdefghi**j**klmnopqrstuvwxyz

J is for **j**ug.
A **j**ug made **j**ust for orange **j**uice.

Trace all of the letters then write your own.

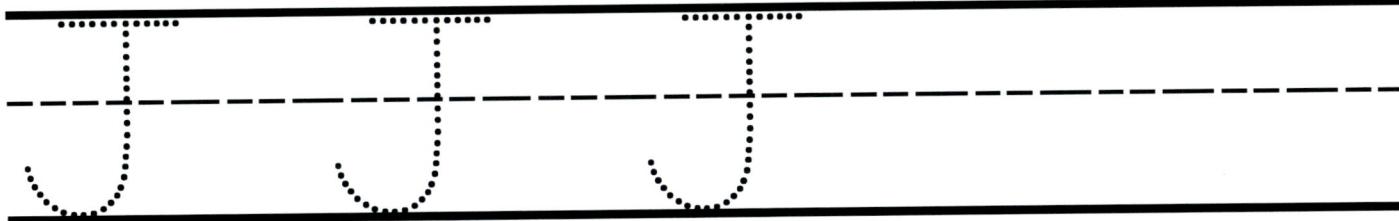

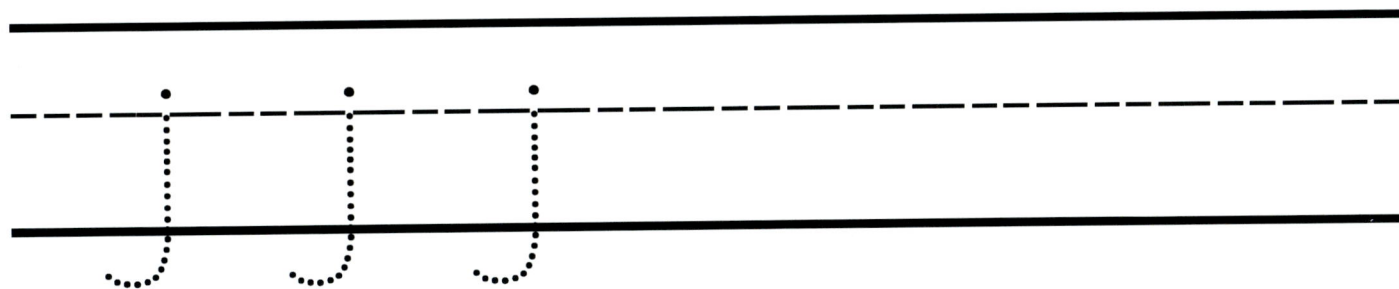

Trace then say the missing letters.

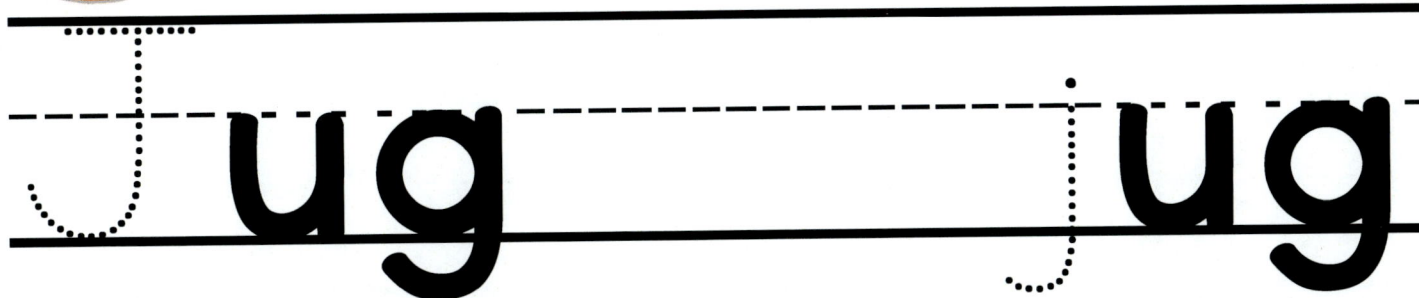

jug jug

ABCDEFGHIJKLMNOPQRSTUVWXYZ

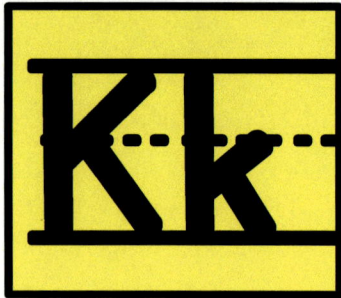

abcdefghijklmnopqrstuvwxyz

K is for kite.
Fly a kite high
up in the sky.

Trace all of the letters then write your own.

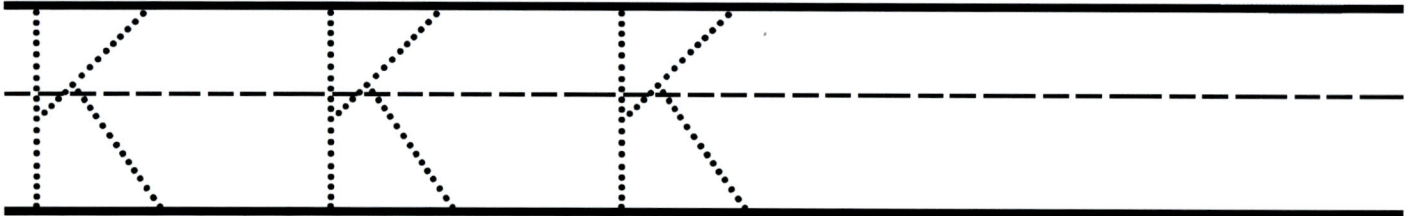

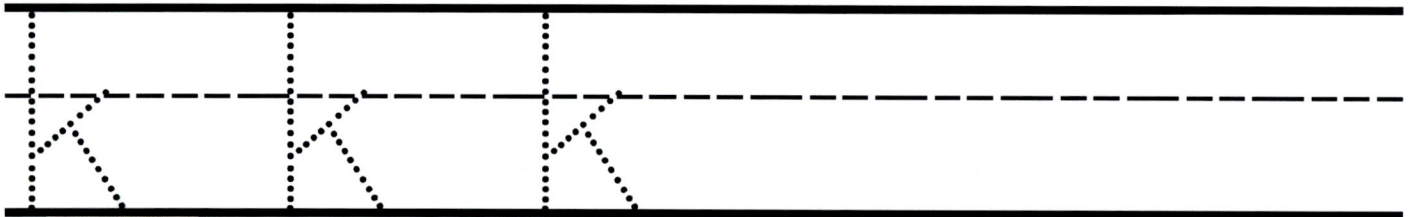

K K K

K K K

Trace then say the missing letters.

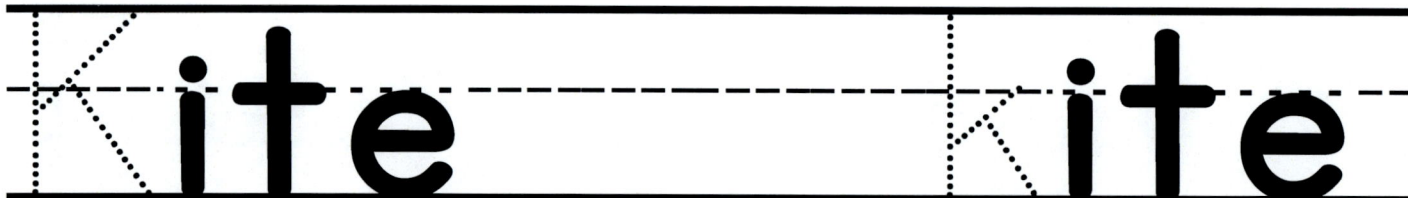

kite   kite

ABCDEFGHIJK**L**MNOPQRSTUVWXYZ

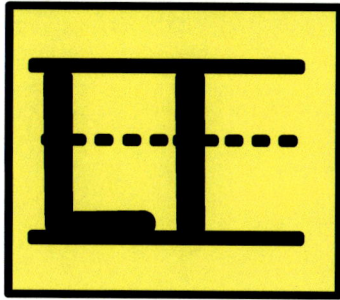

abcdefghijk**l**mnopqrstuvwxyz

L is for **l**eaf.
A **l**eaf fa**ll**ing
from a map**l**e tree.

Trace all of the letters then write your own.

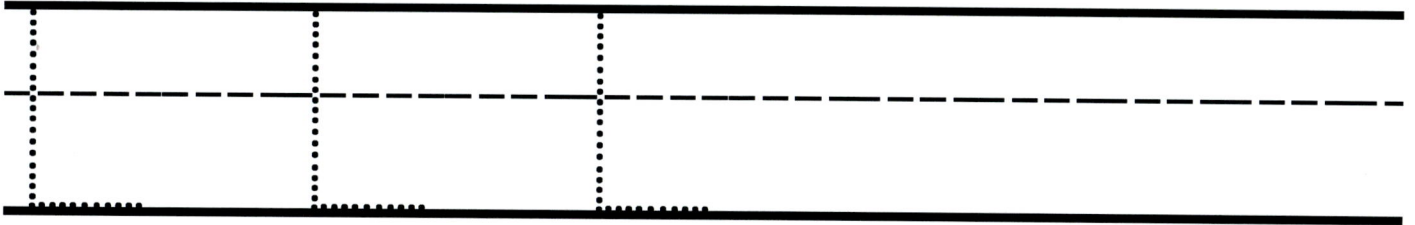

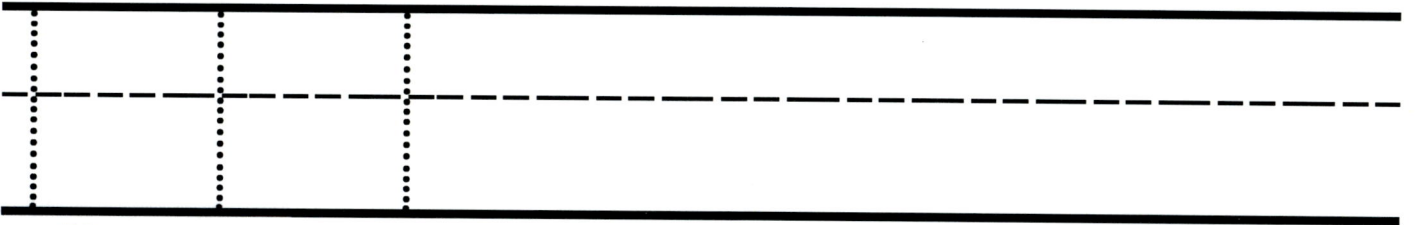

Trace then say the missing letters.

_eaf   _eaf

ABCDEFGHIJKL**M**NOPQRSTUVWXYZ
abcdefghijkl**m**nopqrstuvwxyz

M is for **m**oon.
The **m**an in the
moon has a gno**m**e hat.

Trace all of the letters then write your own.

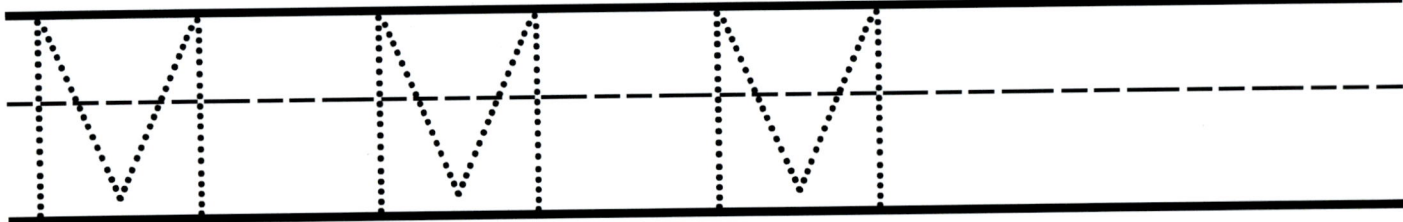

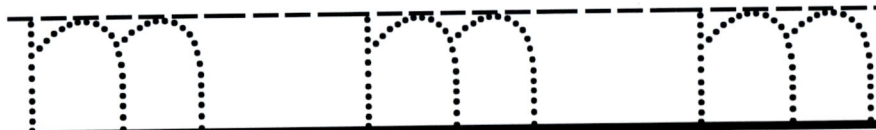

M   M   M   M

m   m   m

Trace then say the missing letters.

Moon   moon

ABCDEFGHIJKLM**N**OPQRSTUVWXYZ

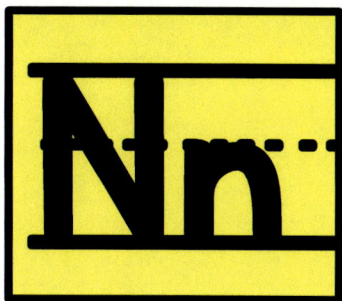

abcdefghijklm**n**opqrstuvwxyz

N is for **N**orma**n**.

Norma**n** **G**nome

k**n**ows a thi**n**g or two.

Trace all of the letters then write your own.

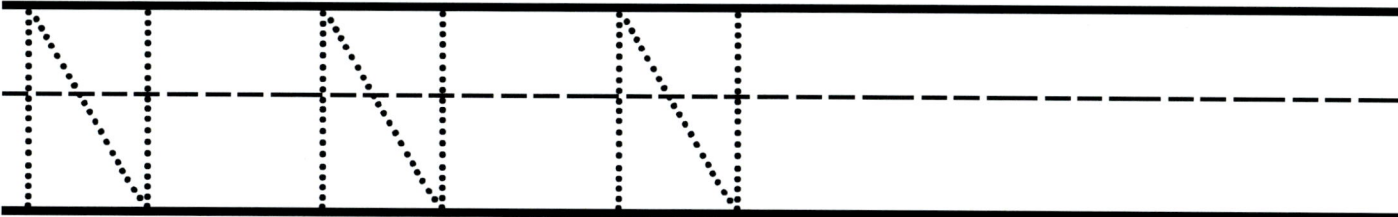

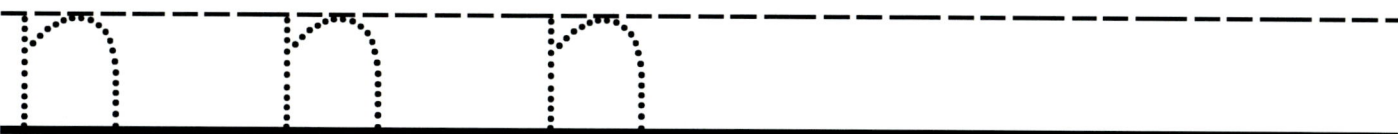

N N N

n n n

Trace then say the missing letters.

Norman

ABCDEFGHIJKLMN**O**PQRSTUVWXYZ

abcdefghijklmn**o**pqrstuvwxyz

O is for **o**ne.

One is m**o**re than zer**o**.

One is less than tw**o**.

Trace all of the letters then write your own.

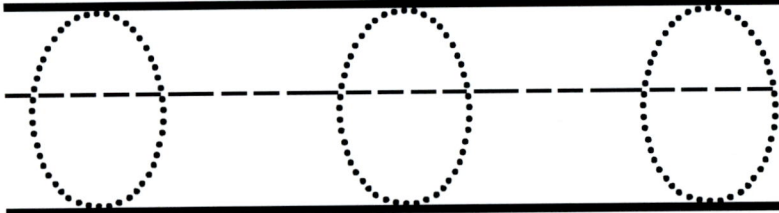

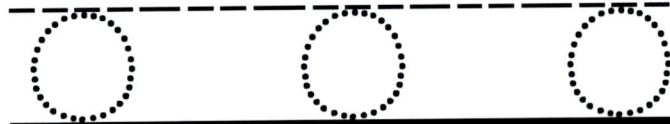

Trace then say the missing letters.

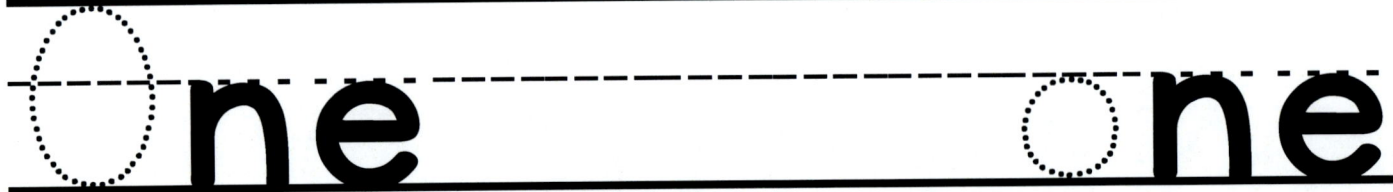

One one

ABCDEFGHIJKLMNOPQRSTUVWXYZ

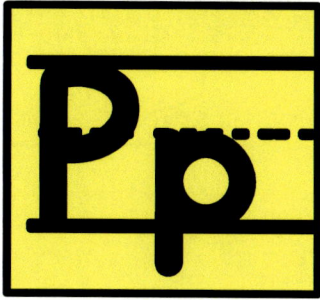

abcdefghijklmnopqrstuvwxyz

P is for **p**igs.
Pink **p**igs play
in a **p**en.

Trace all of the letters then write your own.

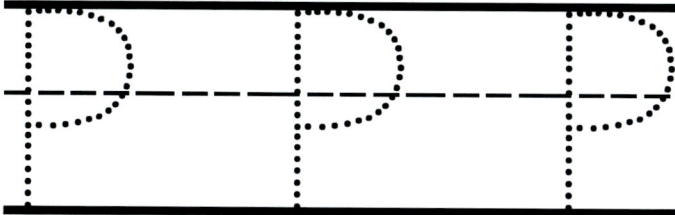

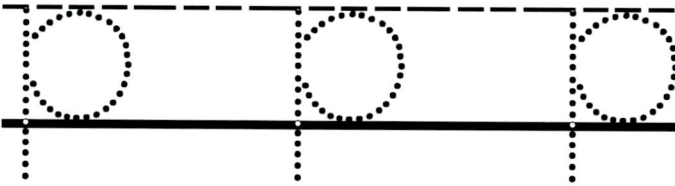

P   P   P

p   p   p

Trace then say the missing letters.

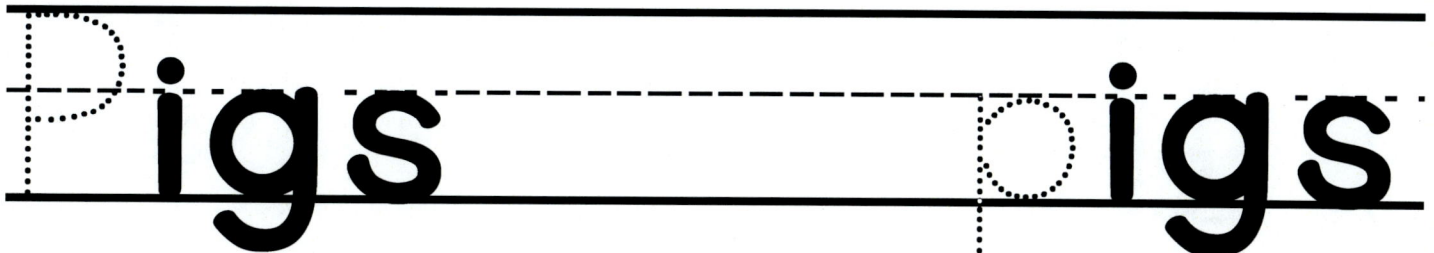

Pigs   pigs

ABCDEFGHIJKLMNOP**Q**RSTUVWXYZ

abcdefghijklmnop**q**rstuvwxyz

Q is for **Q**ueen.

Queen **Q**uilla wears a classy crown.

Trace all of the letters then write your own.

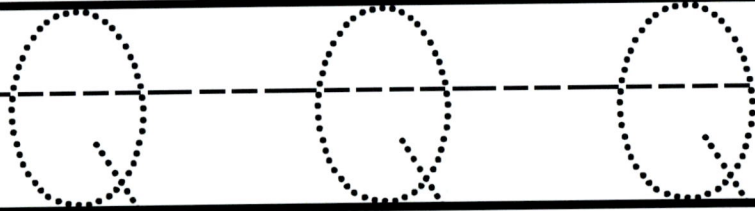

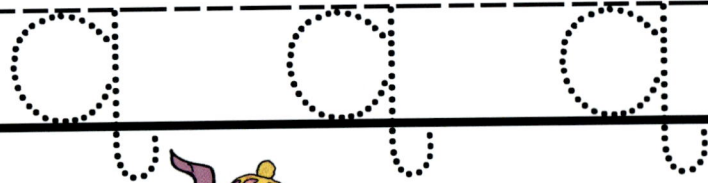

Q   Q   Q

q   q   q

Trace then say the missing letters.

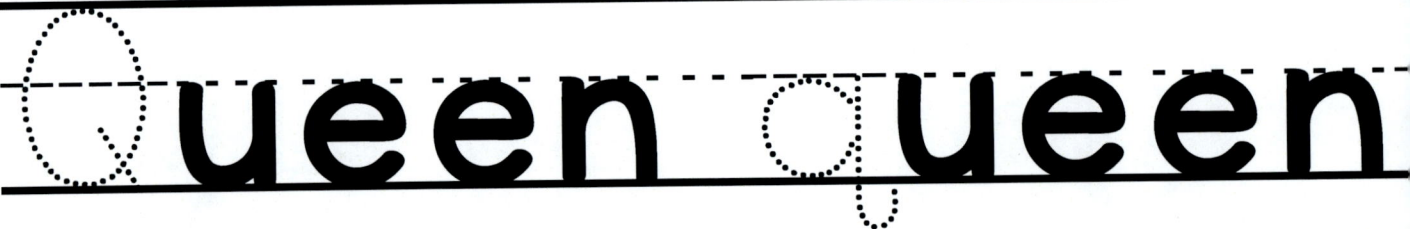

Queen queen

ABCDEFGHIJKLMNOPQRSTUVWXYZ

abcdefghijklmnopqrstuvwxyz

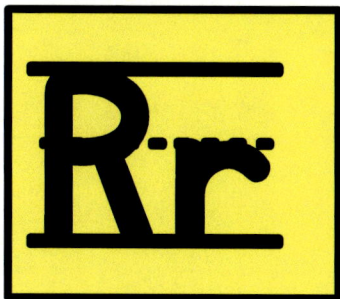

R is for **r**ock.
A b**r**own **r**ock in
the di**r**ty di**r**t.

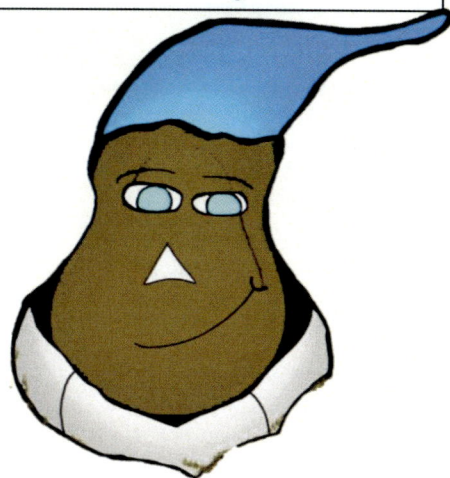

Trace all of the letters then write your own.

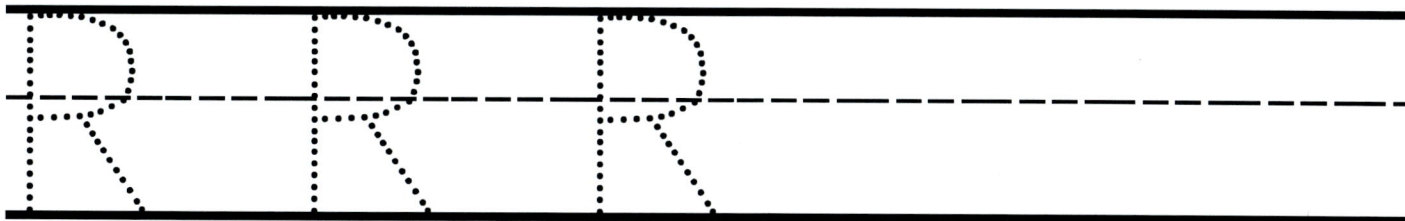

Trace then say the missing letters.

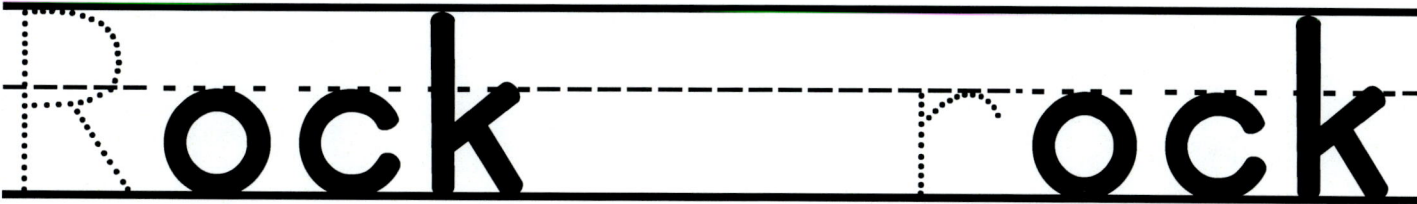

ABCDEFGHIJKLMNOPQR**S**TUVWXYZ

abcdefghijklmnopqr**s**tuvwxyz

S is for **s**top.

Alway**s** **s**top for gnome**s**.

STOP
FOR
GNOMES

Trace all of the letters then write your own.

S S S

s s s

STOP
FOR
GNOMES

Trace then say the missing letters.

Stop   stop

ABCDEFGHIJKLMNOPQRS**T**UVWXYZ
abcdefghijklmnopqrs**t**uvwxyz

T is for trees.
Tiny trees
scattered all about.

Trace all of the letters then write your own.

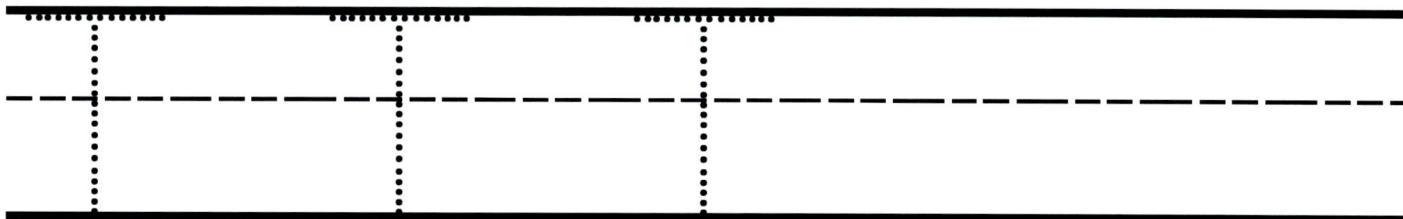

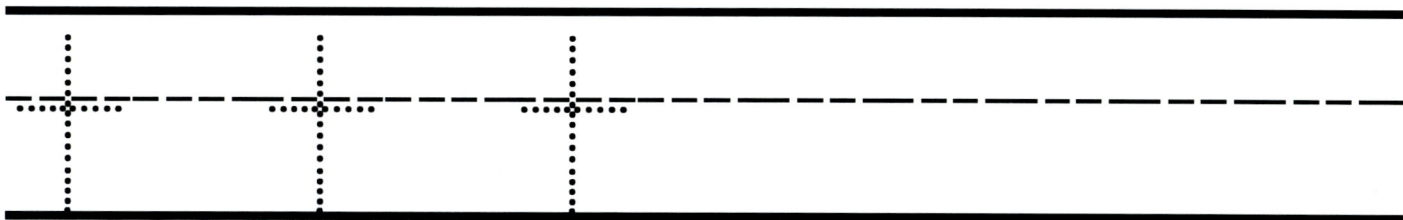

Trace then say the missing letters.

Trees Trees

ABCDEFGHIJKLMNOPQRST**U**VWXYZ

abcdefghijkrst**u**vwxyz

U is for **u**pon.

A sl**u**g sits
upon a st**u**mp.

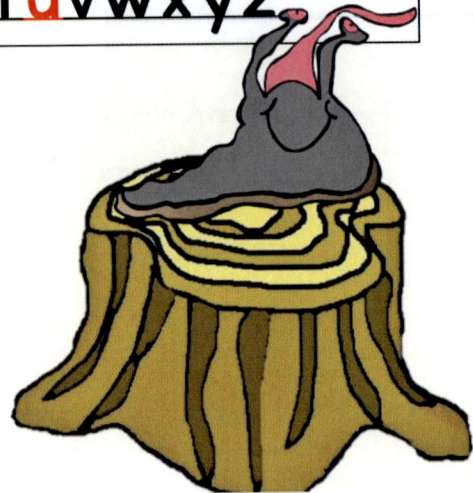

Trace all of the letters then write your own.

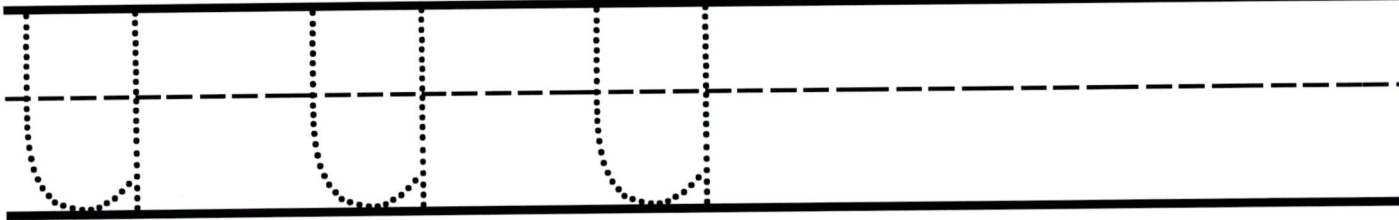

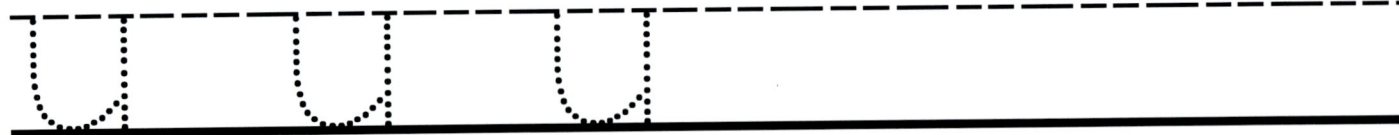

Trace then say the missing letters.

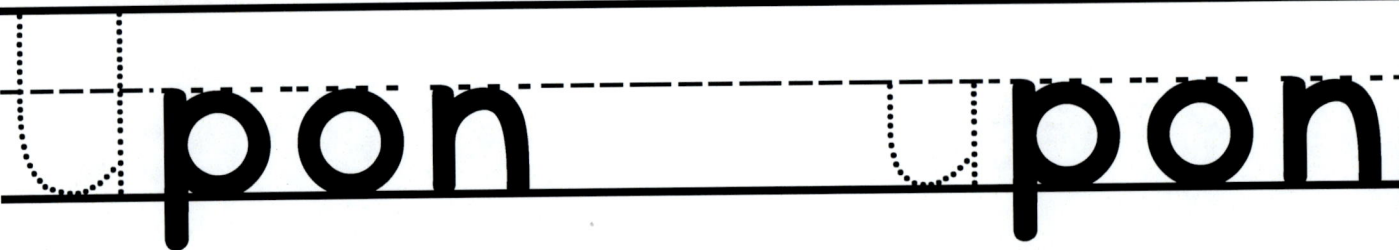

upon **u**pon

ABCDEFGHIJKLMNOPQRSTU**V**WXYZ

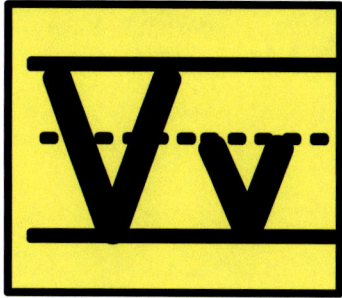

abcdefghijklmnopqrstu**v**wxyz

V is for **v**ase.

A lo**v**ely **v**ase
of potted **v**iolets.

Trace all of the letters then write your own.

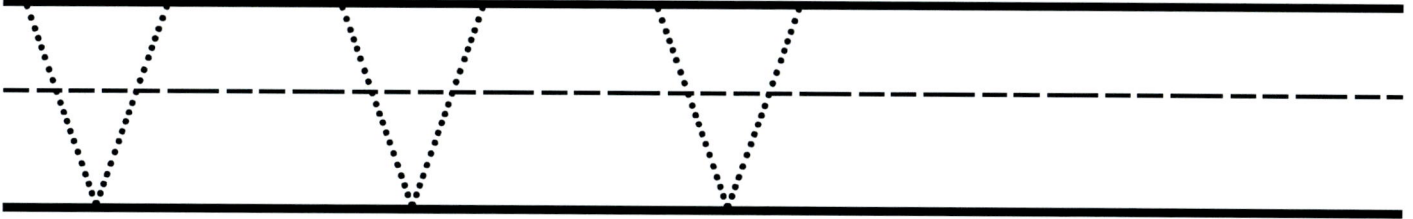

Trace then say the missing letters.

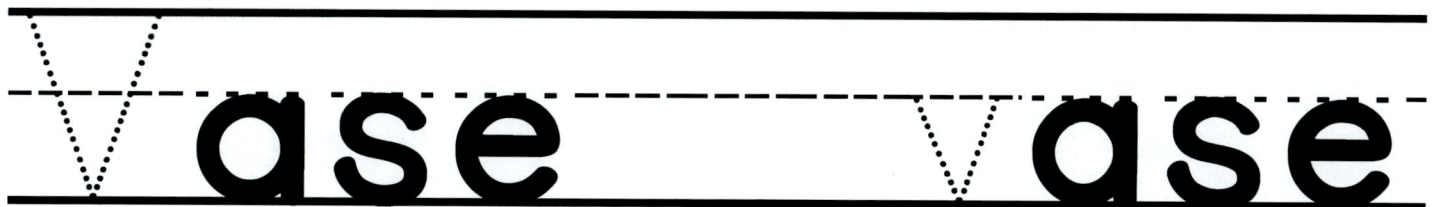

vase **v**ase

ABCDEFGHIJKLMNOPQRSTUVWXYZ

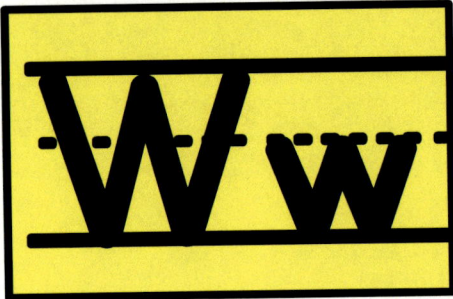

abcdefghijklmnopqrstuvwxyz

W is for worm.
A wee wiggly
white worm.

Trace all of the letters then write your own.

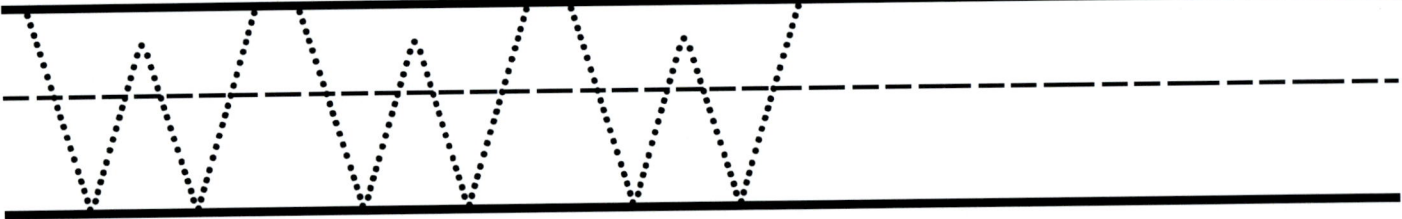

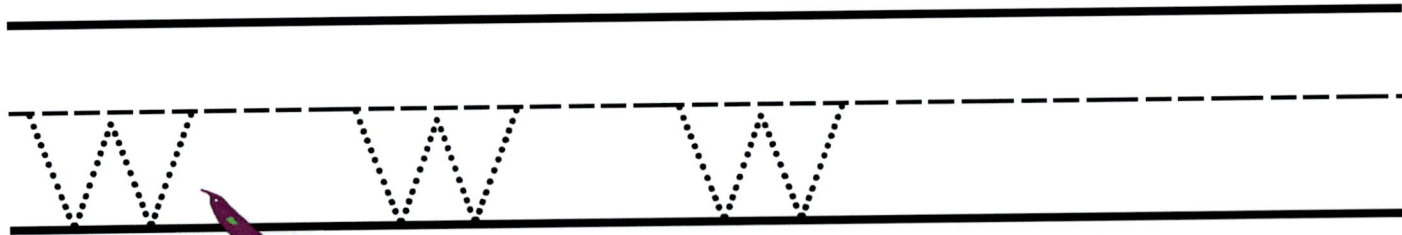

WWWW

W W W

Trace then say the missing letters.

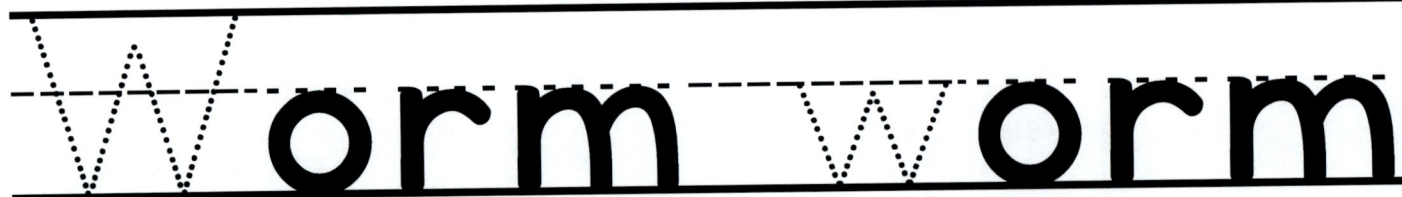

Worm worm

ABCDEFGHIJKLMNOPQRSTUVW**X**YZ

abcdefghijklmnopqrstuvw**x**yz

X x

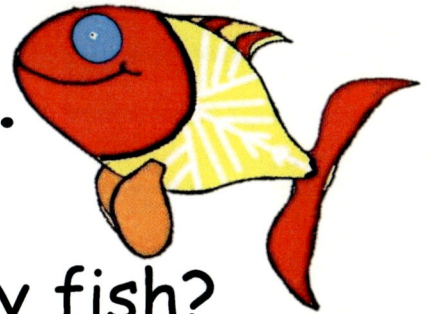

X is for **x**-ray.
Can you see the
bones in the **x**-ray fish?

Trace all of the letters then write your own.

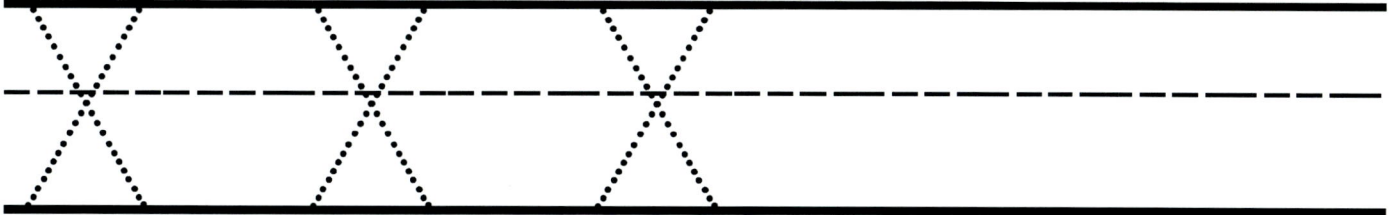

X   X   X

X   X   X

Trace then say the missing letters.

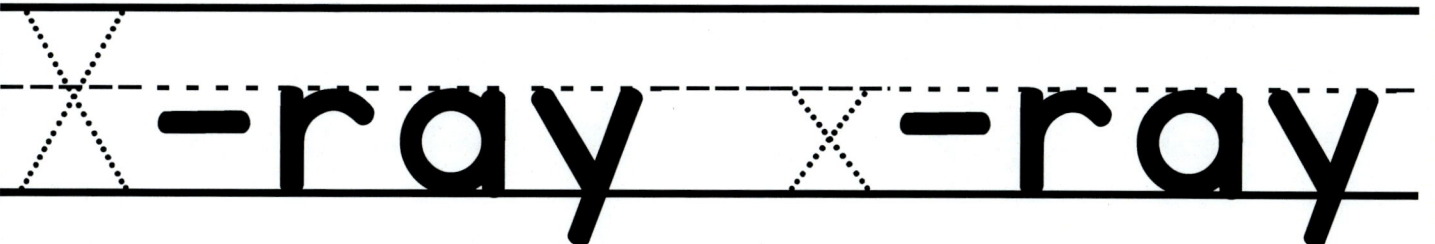

X-ray X-ray

ABCDEFGHIJKLMNOPQRSTUVWXYZ

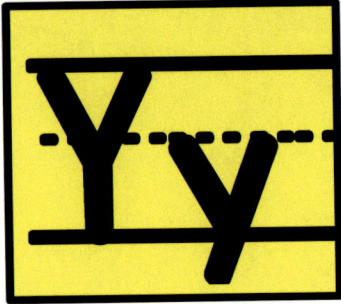

abcdefghijklmnopqrstuvwxyz

Y is for **y**ellow.
Sunn**y** **y**ellow is
the happ**y** sun.

Trace all of the letters then write your own.

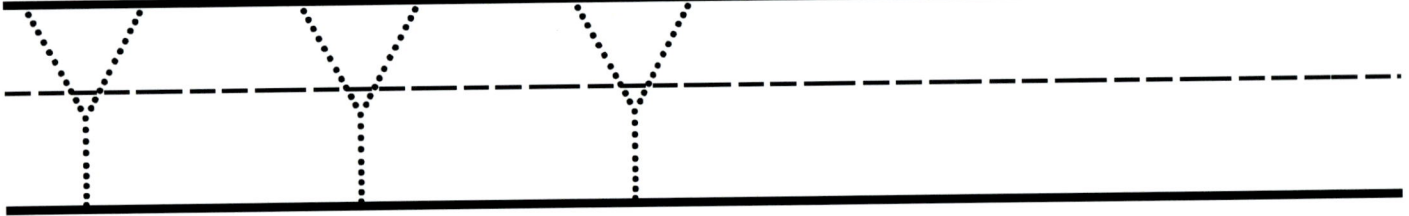

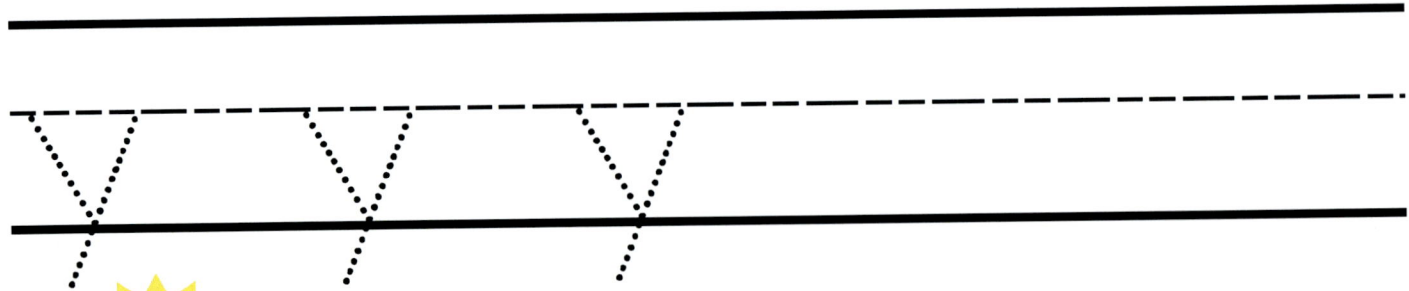

Y Y Y

Y Y Y

Trace then say the missing letters.

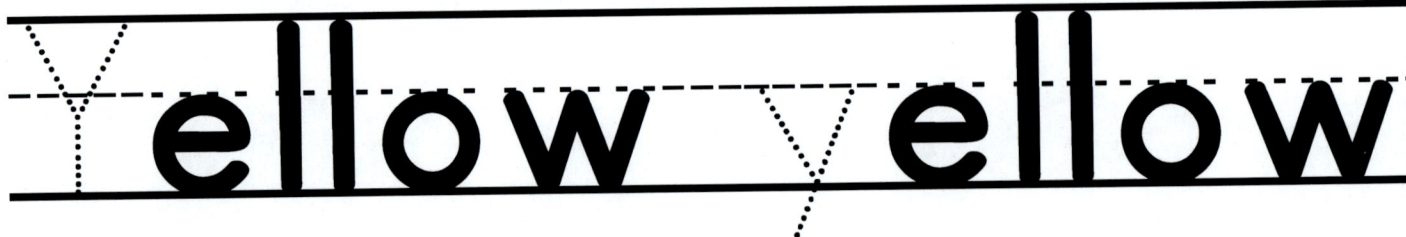

Yellow yellow

ABCDEFGHIJKLMNOPQRSTUVWXYZ

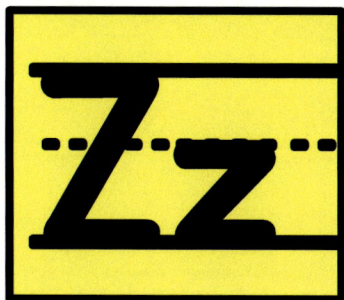

abcdefghijklmnopqrstuvwxyz

Z is for **z**ero.
Zero is one less
than one. **Z**ero.

Trace all of the letters then write your own.

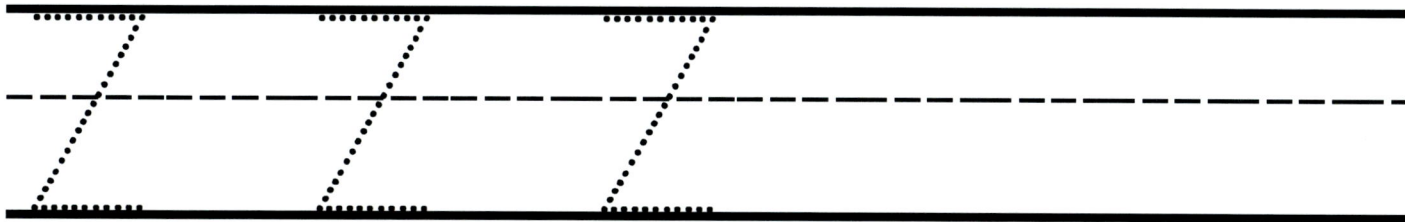

Trace then say the missing letters.

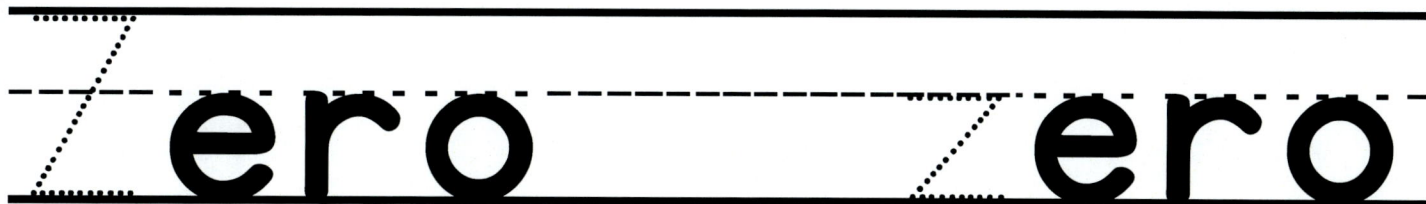

Zero   Zero

B I A J E O

lf

ug

at

nt

ne

ce

top

pon

igs

ase

orm

oon

Jill ❤ Marianne ❤ Paula ❤ Roberta ❤ GG's

Made in the USA
Las Vegas, NV
13 April 2022

47376326R10026